IF I CAN COOK IT,

SO CAN YOU!

❧ ERIK VAN UDEN ❦

AuthorHouse™
1663 Liberty Drive
Bloomington, IN 47403
www.authorhouse.com
Phone: 1 (800) 839-8640

Published by AuthorHouse 07/21/2015

ISBN: 978-1-5049-2331-6 (sc)
ISBN: 978-1-5049-2334-7 (e)

Print information available on the last page.

This book is printed on acid-free paper.

authorHOUSE®

✦ Skillet Corn ✦

Ingredients:

2 Cans of whole kernel sweet corn drained	Cilantro
1 Yellow bell pepper	Olive Oil
1 Orange bell pepper	Butter

Directions:

1) In a large skillet add 2 cans of the drained corn with a tbs of Olive oil

2) Diced the bell peppers and add to the corn

3) Mix well

4) Cook on medium heat for 20 mins stirring occasionally

5) Add a tsp of butter

6) Chop and dice cilantro (about a small handful) and mix together

7) Cook an addition 5 mins on medium high heat

8) Serve and enjoy!

Tip: A great side dish to anything off the grill!

☙ Broccoli with a twist ❧

This is an easy yet different side dish that you and your guests will enjoy. Everyone is used to steamed broccoli but this simple change is something different and a crowd pleaser.

Ingredients:

    2 Crowns of broccoli bunches

    Toasted Sesame Olive Oil

    Pine nuts

    1 Lemon wedge

Directions:

    1) In a large skillet turn to high heat and get piping hot

    2) Add the broccoli crowns

    3) Cook for 1 mins stirring occasionally and turn to medium heat

    4) Add about 5-6 Tbs of the toasted olive oil and mix

    5) Cook on medium heat for 5 mins stirring occasionally

    6) Add about ¼ cup water

    7) Continue cooking until the broccoli softens up

    8) Add a handful of pine nuts

    9) Drizzle one lemon wedge over broccoli and stir together.

Enjoy!

❯‖ Erik's Famous Potatoes ‖❮

Ingredients:

  8 Small red potatoes

  2 Packages lipton soup French onion dip

  1tsp Garlic powder

  2tbs Olive oil

Directions:

1) Cut potatoes into small squares/cubes
2) Add to baking dish
3) Cover potatoes with 2 packages of the onion dip mix
4) Sprinkle garlic powder over potatoes
5) Add olive oil
6) Mix all together
7) Bake on 375 degrees for 45 mins stirring every 15 mins.

Tip: If you find the potatoes drying out while cooking add a touch more olive oil.

⊰╣ Corn Casserole ╠⊱

Ingredients:

   1 (15 ¼ ounce) Can whole kernel corn, drained

   1 (14 ¾ ounce) Can cream style corn

   1 (8 ounce) Package Jiffy corn muffin mix

   1 Cup sour cream

   ½ Stick butter melted

   1 and 1/4th Cup shredded cheddar cheese

Directions:

Pre heat oven to 350 degrees F. In a large bowl, mix the 2 cans of corn,muffin mix, sour cream,and melted butter together. Pour into a 9x13 inch casserole dish. Bake for 45 mins. Remove from oven and top with the cheddar cheese. Return to oven and bake another 5 mins or until the cheese is melted. Serve warm.

Pulled Pork Slider

Ingredients:

2 lbs of Pork tenderloin

1 Bottle of your favorite bbq sauce

6 oz of Dr Pepper or root beer

1 tbs Red pepper flakes

1 tsp Salt

1 tsp Pepper

Slider buns

Directions:

In a crock place the pork into the pot on low heat. Proceed to pour the entire bottle of bbq sauce on top of the pork. Add the red pepper flakes, salt and pepper. Cover and let cook for 1-2 hours. Remove lid and add your Dr pepper or root beer. (your preference in taste) Cover and cook an additional 4 hours. At this time the pork should start to break apart. Remove lid andcut the pork until it comes shredded. Mix the sauce and the pork together, combining well.

Cook an additional 30 mins. Serve on slider buns with your favorite toppings.

Tip:

These are great for appetizers at a get together or party. Always a hit! Grill the buns for a couple of minutes on the grill for a crunchy taste.

Erik's Lemon Chicken

Ingredients:

2 Large chicken breasts	Bread crumbs
6 Lemons	1 Cup flour
Angel hair pasta	1 Egg
Tsp Basil	2 tbs Olive oil

Directions:

1) Place chicken breast in a zip lock plastic bag and squeeze lemon juice from 2 lemons. Let sit/marinate for 30 mins.

2) Whip the egg to a puree in a bowl. Set aside

3) Coat chicken breast each side with flour

4) Dip chicken into egg wash coating each side

5) Coat each side of chicken with bread crumbs

6) Start boiling the angel hair pasta

7) In a large skillet cook chicken on medium/medium high about 4 mins per side until cooked with 2 tbs olive oil and one fresh squeezed lemon

8) While cooking squeeze lemon juice on each side of the chicken breasts

9) Transfer chicken breast to a plate

10) When pasta is cooked and ready to serve, squeeze half a lemon over the pasta

Serve and enjoy! ** Tip. If you have any "crunchy" or leftover breadcrumbs, mix into pasta for some extra flavor. Add lemon juice to your liking

Chicken & Dumplings in a Crock Pot

Ingredients:

4 Boneless chicken breasts	1 Onion diced
2-3 tbs Butter	1 Package of crescent rolls
2 Cans of cream of chicken soup (10.75 oz)	2 Chicken bouillon cubes

Directions:

1) Add all ingredients into the crock pot except for the biscuit dough

2) Cover and cook for 4 hours on high

3) Add the 2 chicken bouillon cubes to crock pot

4) Reduce temperature to low and cook additional 3 hours

5) Make small dumplings out of the dough. The dough WILL expand about twice the size as it cooks so do not make the dumplings bigger than nickel size

6) Cook until dough is no longer raw in the center. Serve and enjoy!

Tip: I add some Morton's Nature Seasoning to the chicken and some pepper for extra flavor

Baked Mystery Chicken

This is a simple and quick recipe for when you don't have much preparation time. However, you would never know it in the flavor! Even better, it's healthy!

Ingredients:

3-4 Chicken breasts

1 tbs Olive oil

3/4th Soy sauce

1 Cup ketchup

1 Cup honey

2-3 Garlic cloves minced

Salt and pepper

Directions:

1) Preheat oven to 350 degrees
2) Place chicken breasts in a 9x13 baking dish
3) Mix together all the ingredients and pour over the chicken
4) Bake for 45 mins to an hour until the sauce is caramelized.

Tip: add a few dashes of red pepper flakes into the mixture if you like spice. Pairs well with white rice or corn.

❧ EVU's Specialty Burgers ❦

Ingredients:

2 lbs Ground chuck hamburger

Season salt (either seasonall or Emeril's Hamburg seasoning)

Cheddar cheese (1 cup)

Worchester sauce

Maple syrup

Directions:

1) In a large mixing bowl add the hamburger meat and cheddar cheese. Mix together

2) Sprinkle a decent amount of the seasoning you chose. Combine in the hamburger

3) Add 1.5 tbs of worchestire sauce and mix together with the meat

4) Combine 2 tbs of maple syrup and form hamburger patties

5) Pre heat grill at 350 degrees

6) Cook patties on the top rack of the grill only flipping one time.

7) Add a dime size squirt of maple syrup on top of each patty

8) Close cover and cook until the meat temperature you desire

9) Add your favorite condiments (cheese, bacon, etc)

10) Enjoy!

Tip: you can add bacon bits in the meat mixture if you're a bacon lover

✢ Honey Sesame Chicken ✢

Ingredients:

4 Boneless chicken breasts

1 & 1/4th Cup honey

½ Cup soy sauce

½ Cup diced onion

¼ Cup ketchup

2 Cloves minced garlic

2 tbs Olive oil

Red pepper flakes

Sesame seeds

White rice

Salt & pepper

Directions:

Season the chicken breasts on both sides with some salt and pepper and place into the crock pot. In a separate bowl combine all the ingredients except for the red pepper flakes. Pour over the chicken. Cook on low heat for 3 hours. Add a few dashes (or more) of red pepper flakes depending on your spice tolerance. Stir. Cook for another hour. Remove lid and top chicken with some sesame seeds. Serve over white rice.

Tip:

For thicker sauce, the last 10 mins of cook time add a tbs of cornstarch with a dash of water and mix. I cut up the chicken, mix it all together with the rice, add some sauce from the pot and your good to go. Enjoy!

⤖ SLLooooow Cook that Chili! ⥈

Ingredients:

1 tbs Vegetable oil	1 tsp Salt
1 Onion diced small	1 tsp Pepper
1 Red bell pepper	1 (28 oz) Can diced tomatoes
4 Garlic cloves minced	1 (14 oz) Can tomato sauce
2 tbs Chili powder	2 Cans (15 oz) light or dark kidney beans drained
1 tbs Ground cumin	1 tsp Soy sauce
1 Pound ground beef OR turkey	1 tbs Brown sugar

Directions:

1) In a skillet, add onions, pepper and garlic over medium heat with some oil for 2-3 mins

2) Add the cumin and chili powder and stir to combine

3) Add the beef or turkey and gook for 5-6 mins stirring occasionally . Drain the grease

4) Add the mixture to the slow cook on low heat. Stir in the brown sugar, soy sauce, tomato sauce, diced tomatoes, and kidney beans.

5) Cover and cook on low for 8 hours.

6) Remove cover, add some salt and pepper and mix.

7) Serve with shredded cheddar cheese, sour cream or jalapenos!

Baked Mozzarella Chicken

Ingredients:

3 Boneless chicken breasts

3 Slices of mozzarella cheese

3 Slices of ham

Sundried tomato strips

Few dashes of oregano

1 Cup flour

1 Cup milk

1 Egg

Some olive oil

Tomato sauce

Directions:

1) Pre heat oven to 320 degrees.

2) Flatten chicken breasts with a meat mallet

3) Salt and pepper both sides

4) Add a few dashes of oregano to one side of each breast

5) Place 4-5 strips of sundried tomato on your chicken breasts

6) Add one slice of ham on top of the tomato strips

7) Add one slice of mozzarella cheese on top of the ham at the end of the breast

8) Roll the chicken from the cheese end and hold together with a toothpick

9) In a separate bowl, whisk the egg with 1 cup of milk.

10) Flour each chicken breasts

11) Transfer to the egg mix to coat

12) Roll in some breadcrumbs to coat each side of the chicken

13) Transfer to a skillet and cook on medium heat with some olive oil to brown each side

14) Remove and bake in pre heated oven for 25-30 mins

15) While the chicken is cooking heat some tomato sauce in a bowl

16) Remove chicken when done and pour some tomato sauce over the chicken

TIP:

If your ham slices are cut sandwich thin, I would add 2 pieces of ham instead of one. This pairs well with a side of zucchini or asparagus.

⇥ Mom's Pot Roast ⇤

Ingredients:

3-5 lbs of Boneless chuck roast

1 Package of ranch dry dressing

1 Package of beef gravy mix

1 Package of French onion soup mix

Small carrots

1 Large onion cut into strips

3 Red potatoes

1 Can of beef broth

Directions:

Using a large crockpot, turn the heat on low. Cut the potatoes into square cubes. Boil the potatoes and carrots on the stove top for about 10-15 mins to soften them up. Add to the crock pot. Combine all the ingredients except for the beef. Stir and mix together well. Add the beef to the crockpot. Cover and cook on low heat for 7-8 hours.

Tip:

You can use a tenderloin instead of the chuck roast if you prefer. The cost of the meal will be higher but some people think the extra tenderness is well worth the extra money. One way to find out is to try the recipe both ways!

❧ Chicken Saltimbocca ❧

Ingredients:

3-4 Boneless chicken breasts	1 Cup white wine
3-4 Sage leaves	1/4th Cup cooking sherry
1 Garlic clove	Few springs of parsley
3-4 Slices of prosciutto	Flour

Directions:

1) Pound the chicken breast to flatten some. Place a piece of prosciutto on each chicken breast.

2) Place a sage leave in the middle of the breast and hold together with a toothpick

3) Lightly flours each side of the chicken breast

4) In a large skillet add some olive oil and brown the chicken on high heat for 2-3 mins with the sage face down on the skillet. Flip over and cook an additional 1-2 mins.

5) Remove the chicken from the skillet and place on a plate. Turn the heat to medium

6) Add the white wine, garlic, sherry and some parsley to the skillet

7) Return the chicken to the skillet and turn to medium high heat and cook for a couple of mins while basting the chicken in the pan juices.

8) Remove and plate. Don't forget to remove the toothpicks before serving!

⇥ Teriyaki Flank Steak ⇤

Ingredients:

  ¼ Cup of Teriyaki Sauce

  1-1½ lbs of Flank steak

  5 tbs Honey

  1 Lime

  ¼ tsp of Red pepper flakes

Directions:

In a bowl place the flank steak and coat in the teriyaki sauce. Cover and refrigerate for one hour. In a small bowl, combine the honey and pepper flakes. Once combined, squeeze a lime wedge into the sauce and stir. On the top rack of the grill cook the steak on medium heat for 5 minutes. Brush the steak with the sauce mixture. Flip the steak and brush with the mixture again. Cook for another 5 minutes. Remove from grill and enjoy!

Tip:

You can use the sauce mixture on any type of steak, chicken, or even pork.

❧ Honey Garlic Pork Chops ❧

Ingredients:

¼ Cup soy sauce

¼ Cup honey

4 Cloves garlic, minced

4-6 Boneless pork chops, trimmed of fat

Directions:

In a bowl, mix the soy sauce, honey, and the garlic together. Coat the pork chops in the mixture. Toss on the UPPER rack on the grill on medium high heat. Close the lid and cook for 5 minutes. Open the lid and baste with a little more honey. Close the lid and cook additional 5 mins or until preferred temperature.

Tip:

If you prefer a little sweeter taste, add 2 tbs of brown sugar to the mixture.

⊁ Too Easy Grilled Ham ⬿

This is such a simple recipe and very inexpensive but will be very popular with your peers or family. I cooked it when I get home from work because it's quick yet delicious.

Ingredients:

2 Fresh cut pieces of ham sliced thick from your local
grocery deli. About the width of your ring finger.

I Can of pineapple slices

Brown sugar

Directions:

1) The day you're going to make the ham coat each side of the ham with brown sugar. Place on a plate. Add 2-3 slices of pineapple on each ham. This will make a marinade of some sort. Keep in fridge until ready to cook.

2) Pre heat your grill to medium heat. Around 350 degrees. Place the slices (with pineapple on) on the top rack of the grill for 5 mins, and then transfer to bottom rack.

3) Take pineapple slices off the ham and cook on grill until you see a grill mark on them, and then transfer back on top of ham. When the ham has some grill marks, plate and serve!

Tip: I serve with Au gratin potatoes and it's a great compliment

⊰ Yummy Marinara Sauce in a Crock Pot ⊱

Ingredients:

2 (28 oz) Cans of crushed tomatoes	1 tbs Brown sugar
1 6 0z Can of tomato paste	1 tbs Balsamic vinegar
1 Yellow onion	1 tbs Oregano
2 Bay leaves	1 tsp Italian seasoning
2 tbs Basil	1 tbs Minced garlic

Directions:

1) Cut the onion and dice it up into small pieces. Add onion and minced garlic to crockpot on low heat and mix together. Add the rest of the ingredients. Stir to combine well.

2) About an hour in add some fresh ground black pepper and some salt. About a tsp each. Continue to cook on low for a total of 7-8 hours.

3) When the cooking time is up remove the 2 bay leaves and stir the sauce. Add salt and pepper to taste. Serve over your favorite pasta and enjoy!

* Tip: If you or adding meatballs or sausage, add to sauce about 6 hours into cooking.

* Tip: This recipe only costs about 50 cents per serving so MUCH cheaper than sauce from the jar!

➤ Chicken & Beef Stir Fry ↞

Ingredients:

2 Chicken breasts

12 oz Top sirloin

Broccoli

Shredded Carrots

1 Small onion

Nature's Seasoning

Stir fry sauce

Directions:

1) In a wok, or large skillet cut the chicken and steak into small cubes.

2) On medium heat brown the chicken on both sides using some olive oil (about 3 mins)

3) Season chicken on both sides with nature's seasoning. Use a decent amount

4) Add the beef cubes and chopped onion. Mix all together

5) Add the stir fry sauce and mix.

6) Add some broccoli florets

7) Reduce heat and continue to cook until your desired steak temperature

8) Add a handful or more of shredded carrots.

9) Mix all together

10) Depending on how "saucy" you like your stir fry, adding some more sauce now is the time

11) Mix all together and serve

Tip: I serve with white or brown rice. Total cook time is about 20 mins so this is quick and easy delicious dish!

⊰ Can't get any easier Chicken Pesto! ⊱

Ingredients:

4 Boneless chicken breasts

1 Jar 6 oz pesto sauce

1 Package of ranch dressing seasoning mix

½ Cup chicken broth

Directions:

In a crock pot turn the temperature to low. Add the chicken broth, pesto, and seasoning mix. Stir well to combine. Add the chicken breast. Cook on high for 3-4 hours or low for 6-8 hours. Serve with angel hair pasta and a vegetable.

Tip:

If your making this meal for 2 people I would use 2-3 chicken breasts and about 4 ounces of pesto and a little less chicken broth. No knives are necessary for this dish, the chicken will fall apart!

CPSIA information can be obtained
at www.ICGtesting.com
Printed in the USA
LVOW05s1618301015

460450LV00014B/52/P